973
POR

Iowa

c/

Steck-Vaughn Company

Executive Editor	Diane Sharpe
Senior Editor	Martin S. Saiewitz
Design Manager	Pamela Heaney
Photo Editor	Margie Foster
Electronic Cover Graphics	Alan Klemp

Proof Positive/Farrowlyne Associates, Inc.
Program Editorial, Revision Development, Design, and Production

Consultant: Dr. Loren N. Horton, Senior Historian, State Historical Society of Iowa

Published by Raintree Steck-Vaughn Publishers, an imprint of Steck-Vaughn Company.

A Turner Educational Services, Inc. book. Based on the Portrait of America television series by R. E. (Ted) Turner.

Cover Photo: State Capitol by © Superstock

Library of Congress Cataloging-in-Publication Data

Thompson, Kathleen.
　　Iowa / Kathleen Thompson.
　　　　p.　cm. — (Portrait of America)
　　"Based on the Portrait of America television series"—T.p. verso.
　　"A Turner book."
　　Includes index.
　　ISBN 0-8114-7335-X (library binding).—ISBN 0-8114-7440-2 (softcover)
　　1. Iowa—Juvenile literature. I. Title. II. Series: Thompson,
Kathleen. Portrait of America.
F621.3.T46　1996
977.7—dc20

　　　　　　　　　　　　　　　　　　　95-30030
　　　　　　　　　　　　　　　　　　　CIP
　　　　　　　　　　　　　　　　　　　AC

Acknowledgments
The publishers wish to thank the following for permission to reproduce photographs:
Pp. 7, 8 © Superstock; p. 10 (both), 11 (both) State Historical Society of Iowa; p. 12 National Museum of Art, Smithsonian Institution; pp. 14, 15 State Historical Society of Iowa; p. 16 The Bettmann Archive; p. 17 (top) National Portrait Gallery, Smithsonian Institution, (bottom) © Jack Zehrt/FPG; p. 18 (both) Reuters/Bettmann; p. 19 © Donovan Reese/Tony Stone Images; pp. 20, 21, 22 (both), 23 State Historical Society of Iowa; p. 24 © Vickie J. Rappe/Iowa Farm Bureau; p. 26 Iowa Farm Bureau; p. 27 © Vickie J. Rappe/Iowa Farm Bureau; p. 28 (top) Maytag, (bottom) John Deere Company; pp. 29, 30 © CVS/Iowa Farm Bureau; p. 31 © Vickie J. Rappe/Iowa Farm Bureau; p. 32 Amana Colonies; p. 34 (top) Living History Farms, (bottom) © IDEA; p. 35 The Bettmann Archive; p. 36 State Historical Society of Iowa; p. 37 © Cathlyn Melloan/Tony Stone Images; p. 38 (left) State Historical Society of Iowa, (right) Art Institute of Chicago; p. 39 Davenport Museum of Art; p. 40 © Ed Sidey; p. 41 (top) TBS, (bottom) © Des Moines Register; p. 42 © Superstock; p. 44 Iowa Department of Education; p. 46 One Mile Up; p. 47 (left) One Mile Up, (center) © Gregory K. Scott/Photo Researchers, (right) © William D. Branford/National Wildflower Research Center.

STECK-VAUGHN

PORTRAIT OF AMERICA

Iowa

Kathleen Thompson

A Turner Book

RSVP

RAINTREE
STECK-VAUGHN
PUBLISHERS

The Steck-Vaughn Company

Austin, Texas

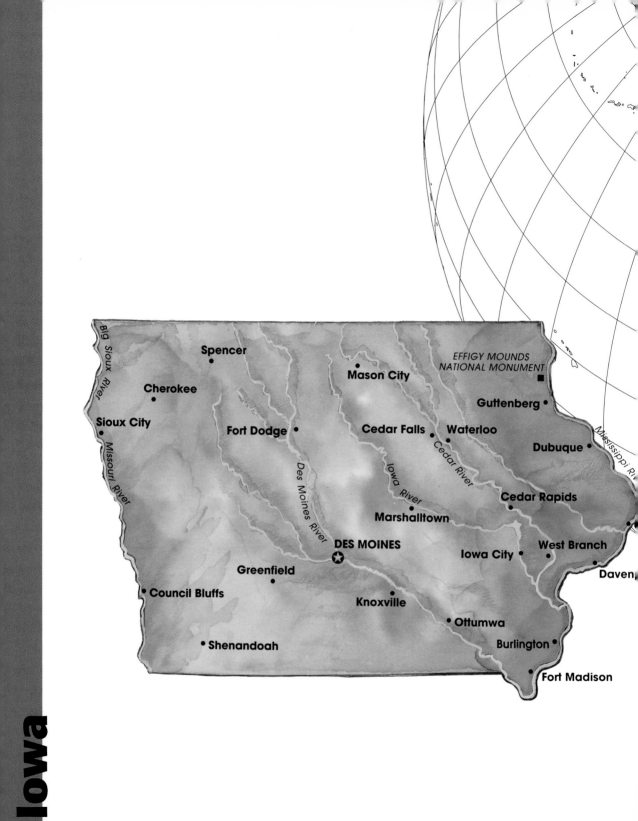

Iowa

Spencer

Cherokee

Sioux City

Fort Dodge

Mason City

Cedar Falls Waterloo

EFFIGY MOUNDS
NATIONAL MONUMENT

Guttenberg

Dubuque

Big Sioux River

Missouri River

Des Moines River

Iowa River

Cedar River

Mississippi River

Cedar Rapids

Marshalltown

DES MOINES

Greenfield

Council Bluffs

Shenandoah

Knoxville

Iowa City

West Branch

Daven

Ottumwa

Burlington

Fort Madison

Contents

Introduction

About a million years ago, glaciers covered Iowa. These huge sheets of ice gathered rich deposits of wind-blown silt called loess. When the ice sheets retreated, the loess was deposited in the remaining shallow valleys, forming some of the richest soil in the world. That's why Iowa is one of the best farming states in America; almost ninety percent of the land is devoted to farming. Iowa produces more than crops, however. It also produces hardworking people. Perhaps Iowa is best represented by Norman Borlaug, who won the Nobel Peace Prize in 1970 for developing ways to help people raise food throughout the world. A true Iowan, Borlaug symbolizes the helpfulness and the farming ability that have made Iowa great.

Iowa farmers conserve their land by contour plowing. The plowed soil creates a barrier that prevents rainwater from washing away the topsoil.

Iowa

ed Delicious apples, hogs, corn

Living Off the Land

About two thousand years ago, people we call the Mound Builders lived in present-day Iowa. The Mound Builders were farmers who grew beans, squash, corn, and other vegetables. These people built earthen mounds to use as burial sites. Many of these mounds, when seen from the sky today, form figures of reptiles, bears, birds, and other animals.

When European explorers arrived in the late 1600s, there were several other Native American groups in the Iowa area. Most lived near one of the area's two rivers, the Mississippi to the east and the Missouri to the west. The largest of the eastern groups was the Iowa people. Other groups that lived along the Mississippi River included Dakota, Sauk, Fox, Illinois, Miami, and Ottawa. The Missouri, Omaha, Oto, and Osage lived in the west. All of these Native American groups had similar lifestyles. They usually lived in teepees, which were cone-shaped homes covered with animal skins. They farmed, fished, and hunted deer and buffalo.

This statue stands outside the Iowa State capitol in Des Moines.

9

The Mound Builders built these animal-shaped mounds. The outlines in the photo show the shapes.

This is what the mounds look like up close.

The French explorers Louis Jolliet and Father Jacques Marquette stopped in the Iowa area in the summer of 1673, on their way down the Mississippi River from Canada. They met briefly with an offshoot group of the Illinois people, called the Peoria, then left to explore the Mississippi farther south.

About ten years later, France claimed all North American land along the Mississippi River basin. France based its claim on a trip explorer René-Robert Cavelier, Sieur de La Salle, made down the Mississippi in 1682. La Salle hadn't explored any of the land area, only the river itself. La Salle named the area Louisiana in honor of the French king Louis XIV. The area now known as Iowa was part of this huge territory.

Over the next 120 years, life changed little for the Native Americans in the Iowa area. Along the Atlantic Coast, the 13 British colonies declared their independence and fought against Great Britain in the Revolutionary War. In 1783 the colonists won the war and established themselves as a new country—the United States of America. Then, in 1803 France sold its claim to the Louisiana Territory to the United States for $15 million. The land area included all the land west of the Mississippi River to the Rocky Mountains. The sale became known as the Louisiana Purchase. President Thomas Jefferson was eager to find out more about the territory he had just bought. In 1804 he sent Meriwether Lewis and William Clark to explore the territory and to look for a water passage to the Pacific Ocean. The Lewis and Clark expedition passed briefly by present-day Iowa on their way up and down the Missouri River.

By the early 1830s, the Iowa area was still mostly unsettled by pioneers. More Native Americans, however, were being pushed into the area to make room for settlement elsewhere. Two Native American groups, the Sauk and the Fox, were forced out of the Illinois area. Leaders of these two groups had signed a

This statue depicts Louis Jolliet. Jolliet, Father Jacques Marquette, and a five-person crew traveled almost all the way down the Mississippi River in two canoes made of birch tree bark.

Julien Dubuque was Iowa's first European American settler. In 1788 he convinced the Fox to allow him to mine lead in the area near present-day Dubuque.

11

This painting of Sauk leader Black Hawk now hangs in the Smithsonian Museum. In 1838 Black Hawk became one of Iowa's first writers. He told his story to a Davenport resident, who wrote it down and had it published.

treaty with the federal government, agreeing to move across the Mississippi River into present-day Iowa. However, many of these Native Americans, such as the Sauk leader Black Hawk, thought the treaty was unfair and wanted to stay on their native land. In 1832 Black Hawk led a group of about one thousand Sauk back to their Illinois land in order to plant spring crops. Black Hawk's party included women, children, and elderly men. The United States forces attacked anyway, starting the Black Hawk War. Black Hawk's warriors won the first battle, but they were soon outnumbered and forced to retreat north to present-day Wisconsin. The United States forces met them at the Bad Axe River and killed almost the entire group.

To punish the Sauk and the Fox for breaking the treaty, Congress forced them to sign a second treaty, giving up some of their Iowa land. The other remaining Native American groups in this area, appalled by the slaughter of Black Hawk's followers, began to move west to avoid more trouble with the United States troops. Most Native Americans had left the Iowa area by the 1840s.

The fifty-mile strip of Iowa land that the Sauk and the Fox had been forced to give up was called the Black Hawk Purchase. The land was first made part of the Michigan Territory. Then Congress shifted it to the Wisconsin Territory when that territory was created in 1836. Congress at last created the Iowa Territory in 1838. This huge territory stretched to the Canadian border. It included parts of today's Minnesota, North Dakota, and South Dakota. Its first federal census counted 43,112 settlers.

Iowa's present boundaries were at last defined in December 1846, when it became the twenty-ninth state. Congress admitted Iowa at the same time as Florida, to balance the number of states that allowed slavery with the number that didn't. Florida allowed slavery, and Iowa did not.

The last of Iowa's Native American conflicts took place in 1857, the same year the state adopted its constitution. Although no Native American groups lived in Iowa by this time, some groups still traveled to hunt in their former territory. In March 1857 a group of Sioux returned to Spirit Lake in northwest Iowa. When they saw settlers living around the lake, which they still considered a sacred area, they became angry. The Sioux attacked the settlement for five days, killing over thirty people. However, the attack did not discourage other settlers from coming to Iowa. They continued to arrive in large numbers.

That same year one Native American group returned peacefully to their former Iowa land. The Fox had been moved to a reservation in Kansas. Six years later they bought back a small plot of their former land from the government for one thousand dollars. That price was 125 times more than the government had paid the Fox for the land when they were forced to

This photo shows the Mississippi River along the Iowa border in the mid-1800s, the height of the logging days.

leave it. Over time the Fox raised enough money to expand their land to three thousand acres.

By 1860 Iowa's population had reached almost 675,000. Around this time the friction between the North and the South over the slavery issue was reaching its peak. Southern states argued that slavery was necessary for their economy. Cotton was the most important crop in the South, and owners needed slaves to work on their cotton plantations. The Northern states, which did not have cotton plantations, said slavery was cruel and unjust. Northerners quoted the Declaration of Independence, which stated that all men were created equal. Iowa's southern neighbor Missouri allowed slavery, and many Missouri slaves tried to escape to Iowa. Those that managed to cross the border still were not considered free, however. Federal law stated that escaped slaves had to be returned to their owners. As a result some Iowans became part of the nationwide Underground Railroad. This was a path of homesteads reaching to Canada that provided temporary shelter for fugitive slaves.

In 1861 arguments between the North and the South over slavery, the rights of individual states, and economic issues exploded into the Civil War. The Southern states declared independence from the Union, calling themselves the Confederate States of America. Iowa sent 75,000 soldiers to fight for the Union—a higher percentage of its population than any other state. No Civil War battles were fought in Iowa. The Confederacy surrendered in 1865.

After the war Iowa concentrated on building its economy. Steamboats brought large shipments of logs from Wisconsin and Minnesota down the Mississippi River. The lumber was used to build homes, businesses, and towns. By 1880 Iowa was crisscrossed with more than five thousand miles of railroad tracks. Railroads carried Iowa farmers' goods to consumers across the nation. The steamboats and railroads also brought more people, especially European immigrants moving west from the crowded eastern states. By 1880 the population of Iowa increased to more than 1,600,000.

In 1868 African American men were given the right to vote. In the years that followed, there were several court cases in which the Iowa courts ruled

When Iowa's railroads were completed in 1880, Iowa farmers could ship their goods farther and more quickly. Every farm had a train station not more than 25 miles away.

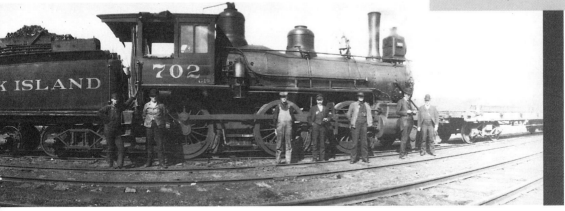

against segregation, or the separation of the races in public places. While battles over segregation in some southern states lasted as late as the 1970s, Iowa had desegregated its schools and other public institutions almost one hundred years earlier.

Iowa also played a leading role in the struggle of women to gain equal rights. In 1869 an Iowa-born woman, Arabella Babb Mansfield, became the first female lawyer in the nation. In the late 1800s, another Iowa native, Carrie Chapman Catt, helped form the Iowa Woman Suffrage Association. This organization worked to gain women the right to vote. Catt became president of the National American Woman Suffrage Association in 1900. In 1920 Catt delivered a crucial speech to Congress that helped to pass the Nineteenth Amendment, granting women the right to vote.

Manufacturing became an important industry in Iowa in the twentieth century. One of the first major manufacturing products in the state was the washing machine, invented by Fred Maytag of Newton. Farm machinery was also produced in Iowa factories. The Schaeffer company began manufacturing pens in Fort Madison around 1910.

When the United States entered World War I in 1917, Iowa's corn was in high demand to feed soldiers overseas. Before he became President in 1929, Iowan Herbert Hoover was in charge of sending food to the Allies and to famine areas in Europe. When the war ended in 1918, however, the prices paid for farm goods fell drastically. Farmers spent the next nine years struggling to survive on lower profits. In the 1930s the entire

Carrie Chapman Catt was a leader of the national women's movement for more than thirty years.

16

nation went into a severe economic slump called the Great Depression. Millions of people lost their jobs, and financial institutions went bankrupt. Thousands of Iowa farmers lost their farms.

The nation's economy began to recover when the United States entered World War II in 1941. Many factories across the nation were contracted by the government to make war materials. Once again soldiers overseas created a large demand for farm products, especially Iowa's corn and livestock. Farmers began to make money again as the agriculture industry grew. Most of Iowa's industry—in food processing, farm machinery, and other manufacturing areas—was directly related to agriculture. Many workers left the farms to find better-paying jobs in the factories. By 1960 more Iowans lived in cities than in rural areas. In the 1970s profits from manufacturing overtook farming profits for the first time.

Iowa farmers struggled again in the 1980s due to an economic condition called inflation. Rising prices

Iowan Herbert Hoover was elected President of the United States one year before the Great Depression began.

During the early to mid-1800s, riverboats were the main form of transportation. Today, they are used mainly as tourist attractions on the rivers that run through Iowa.

made running a farm more expensive, but farmers were not paid any more money for their goods to cover these additional costs. Farms across the state ran out of money. This meant that the factories that made farming goods, such as plows and fertilizers, lost money, too. Many of Iowa's workers, especially young workers, moved out of the state to find jobs.

In the late 1980s, the Iowa state government, with the help of telecommunications companies, devised an innovative way to draw people to the state. Iowa began to build an electronic computer network for its public schools. The hope was that state-of-the-art technology in the classrooms would attract families and businesses. Families would benefit from Iowa's excellent public schools. Businesses would follow because these schools would train a technologically advanced workforce. Today, Iowa's population is one of the best educated in the country.

Disaster struck farmers across the Midwest in 1993. Crops were destroyed by

above. In 1993 Iowans living along the Mississippi River had to build dikes out of sandbags to hold back the flood.

right. When the Mississippi River flooded in 1993, Davenport's Jack O'Donnell Stadium was completely filled with water.

Iowa's largest city, Des Moines, has grown into an important center for the insurance industry. Des Moines is also a regional center for wholesaling, retailing, manufacturing, and publishing.

floods followed by early frost. The federal government estimated that about five hundred thousand acres of farmland were ruined, while a total of 40 million acres were severely damaged. President Bill Clinton declared the entire state of Iowa a disaster area. The federal government set up aid programs to reimburse farmers for their losses. Even with this help, some of Iowa's farmers are not expected to fully recover until the year 2000.

As the nation's biggest cities have become increasingly polluted and crime-ridden, many people find peaceful, uncrowded states such as Iowa attractive. Some experts believe that by the end of the century, Iowa could experience another population boom. New technology that allows more people to work outside of cities could make this possibility a reality. How these changes would affect the state can only be imagined for now.

An Unusual Mining Town

During the years following the Civil War, many southern states passed laws that prevented African Americans from having the same rights and privileges as other citizens. In addition most African Americans could get only poorly paying jobs as farm laborers or domestic servants. Prejudice also existed in the North, where many African Americans worked at low-paying jobs and lived in crowded, segregated areas of cities. The mining community of Buxton, Iowa, was different. African Americans were well-paid, lived in comfortable houses, and experienced very little, if any, racial discrimination.

Consolidation Coal Company established Buxton in 1900. Most coal towns of the late 1800s and early 1900s were located close to the mines. The miners and their families lived in cramped conditions where noise and coal dust were always present. Consolidation, however, placed Buxton farther from the mines than was usual. It also took into account such factors as water supply and the community's potential for growth.

With a population of five thousand, Buxton was larger than most mining towns. Most coal mining towns had populations of around two hundred.

Almost all of Buxton's institutions were racially integrated.

In 1905 African Americans made up 55 percent of Buxton's population. The coal company recruited African Americans on purpose, which was helpful since many African Americans at the turn of the century were desperately looking for work. The rest of the population included people of European descent. From 1900 to 1910, Buxton was Iowa's largest coal-mining community.

Consolidation Coal Company's business philosophy stated that if a company provided services, such as housing, parks, libraries, schools, and recreational facilities, the employees would be satisfied and would work hard for the company. Consolidation built houses that miners rented, operated a huge department store, and built a community center with a swimming pool. The company also paid good wages. Many African Americans were able to earn enough money to open businesses, buy land, and send their children to college.

Consolidation was not the only company to operate its own town. Most companies, though, tried to control the personal lives of the workers in their towns. Some company towns had only one church, which

After the Consolidation Coal Company closed its mines, many close friends were separated as families moved to Des Moines, Waterloo, Cedar Rapids, and even cities outside of Iowa.

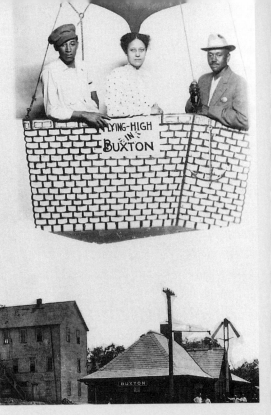

This photo collage expresses the feeling of freedom that many African Americans felt in Buxton.

residents were required to attend. In Buxton, Consolidation allowed workers to form many churches and to attend whichever church they pleased. Consolidation also permitted newspaper editors to criticize the company in the local paper.

While Consolidation's business philosophy was very humanitarian, the company was still in business to make a profit. But that didn't stop the coal company from supporting women whose husbands had been killed in the mines or from aiding employees who were injured on the job. In addition Consolidation paid African American and European American men equal wages for working in the mines. Most companies at that time found excuses to pay African Americans less.

Perhaps because of the company's policy of offering equal pay and equal treatment, many people in Buxton socialized together comfortably. African Americans and European Americans often lived near each other, went to school together, and attended the same social events. African American residents recall that employees who behaved badly toward others were encouraged by the company to move someplace else.

Buxton's prosperity didn't last. Between 1914 and 1917, an explosion closed a mine, and some fires in the town damaged Buxton's economy. Many miners transferred to other Consolidation mines farther away. By 1918 Consolidation had closed all their mines near Buxton. By 1923 everyone had moved away, and the buildings were torn down.

Buxton was a place where African Americans enjoyed a standard of living and a freedom from prejudice that few other African Americans at that time were allowed. For many years after Buxton ceased to exist, hundreds of former residents gathered at reunions to share memories with friends who had lived in the "king of the mining communities." Former resident Marjorie Brown comments regretfully, "Buxton was something else. You can imagine how we grieved for it."

Not all African American men living in Buxton were coal miners. Some were doctors, dentists, lawyers, accountants, teachers, and school principals.

23

Iowa Feeds the World

About ninety percent of the land in Iowa is used for some type of farming. Only Nebraska devotes more land to agriculture. Although manufacturing has brought Iowa more money since the 1970s, agriculture still dominates the state. This is because manufacturing in Iowa is almost entirely related to agricultural products and farm machinery.

Iowa farms generate about ten billion dollars of income for Iowa each year. Almost three billion dollars of that comes from exports to other countries. In fact California is the only state that exports more agricultural products than Iowa. The state outranks all others in world exports of grains and feed.

As far as overall sales go, Iowa is the nation's leading producer of both corn and hogs. Iowa's farmers produce about 1.5 billion bushels of corn and about 14 million hogs each year. That's about one fifth of the nation's corn and one quarter of the nation's pork.

Iowa's livestock products just barely surpass its crop production. About 55 percent of the state's farm

Grain elevators such as this one are making Iowa's farms increasingly modern.

income comes from livestock, and about 45 percent comes from crops. In addition to hogs, sheep and cattle are also important livestock products in Iowa. In fact Iowa ranks in the nation's top five states for production of both sheep and cattle. Dairy cows, chickens, and turkeys are also raised by Iowa's livestock farmers.

Soybeans aren't far behind corn as Iowa's biggest crop. In fact Iowa is the nation's second largest producer of soybeans. Iowa farms grow almost three hundred million bushels of soybeans every year. Only Illinois produces more soybeans than Iowa. As with corn much of the state's soybean harvest is ground into feed for its livestock. Soybeans are also used in making oil, margarine, nondairy cheese, and soy sauce. In addition, soybeans are used in producing nonfood products such as paint, fertilizer, and adhesives.

Iowa farms rank in the nation's top five for oats and alfalfa hay. Fruits and vegetables, although less important than grains, are still widely grown. The Red Delicious apple was developed by an Iowa farmer in the nineteenth century.

Iowa's largest manufacturing activity is food processing. Factories process goods from Iowa's farms and ship them across the country and around the world. Corn is one of Iowa's most important farm crops, and products processed from corn outnumber products from any other source. Iowa food-processing plants produce corn oil, cornstarch, popcorn, corn flakes, and many other products made from corn.

Meat packing, especially sausages and hot dogs, is a major food-processing activity. In 1964 Iowan Ray T. Townsend invented a machine that most factories still use today to stuff and section their sausages and hot dogs. The machine can turn out about thirty thousand links an hour!

Some Iowa plants pasteurize, homogenize, and package milk from Iowa dairy farms. Other plants process milk into other dairy products, such as cheese, yogurt, and cottage cheese. Iowa is the fifth largest cheese producer in the nation. In all well over fifty thousand of Iowa's workers manufacture some type of food product.

Nonelectric machinery is Iowa's second most important manufacturing industry. Perhaps not surprisingly, most of the machinery produced is farm equipment. Iowa's largest employer is the John Deere Company, which makes tractors, harvesters, combines, and other farm machines. Waterloo, Des Moines, and Davenport are some of the major cities

Hog farms are such a big business in Iowa that there are about five times more hogs than people in the state!

Some of the first manufactured products in Iowa were washing machines invented by Fred Maytag of Newton. The Maytag Corporation produces washers and dryers in Iowa to this day.

where this type of manufacturing is done. Almost forty thousand of the state's workers build some type of nonelectric machine.

A third area of Iowa's economy, taken as a whole, produces more money for the state than manufacturing and agriculture combined. Service industries produce about thirty billion dollars for the state each year. Service industries are those in which workers serve other people instead of make an actual product. About one out of every two workers in Iowa has a service job. There are many different types of service industries, but the largest in Iowa are finance, insurance, and real estate, which bring in about ten billion dollars per year. Employees in this category may be bankers, insurance agents, or real estate agents. Des Moines is particularly well-known for its concentration of insurance agencies.

Over 12,000 Iowans help manufacture farm and garden machinery, such as the tractor shown here.

Modern farm methods have allowed farmers to harvest grains faster than ever before.

The next most important category of service industries in Iowa is wholesale and retail trade, which brings in about eight billion dollars a year. Retail trade workers, such as grocery store cashiers, tractor salespeople, and department store clerks, sell products in small quantities. Wholesale trade workers sell large quantities of products, usually to companies. A wholesale trade worker might sell farm goods to food-processing factories or tractors to farm-equipment stores. Almost three quarters of Iowa's trade workers sell grain, farm machinery, and other farm supplies.

Iowa's economy used to be dependent solely on agriculture. This meant that a single bad crop year could make it a bad year for all of Iowa's workers. Today, Iowa's diversified economy, one that has many types of businesses, has shielded the state in case of a disaster, such as the 1993 flood. The state's balanced combination of rich soil and strong industry have helped it maintain one of the healthiest economies in the nation.

Good Neighbors

There's still a lot of open country in Iowa. That means that you can't walk next door to borrow a cup of sugar—because next door may be miles down the road. You might think that people who live so far apart don't get to know each other very well. In fact it's often just the opposite.

A few years ago, Cheryl MacVey needed all the help she could get. She lives on a farm with her husband, Denny, and their two children. Cheryl helps out with the farmwork once in a while, but it's Denny who runs the farm. So when Denny had to go to Virginia for a heart transplant, Cheryl was worried.

It turned out she had nothing to worry about. The MacVeys' neighbors came through for them. They held a community dinner to raise money for the MacVeys. "To us it is just awesome," said Cheryl. "When we found out how many people were there and how much money was raised, we just couldn't believe it. And I think it wasn't so much that we got the money. It was the fact that everybody was thinking about us and helped

Raising and harvesting crops takes a lot of hard, careful work. It requires teamwork, long hours, and the right equipment.

The average farmer produces enough food for eighty people.

us out. And we knew how many people really liked us back here. You know, it just lifted our spirits a lot."

The dinner was just one of the ways the neighbors helped out. They also came in to make sure the farm work got done. Crops don't wait for anything, not even heart transplants.

Tom Eberle was one of the neighbors helping the MacVeys. When he agreed to take over most of their farm work while Denny was in the hospital, he didn't think he was doing anything special. "I know the neighbors would come into my place just like I've come here," said Eberle. "And the other neighbors have all helped. That's just the way it's always been in this area.

Oh, you worry about the weather and all the conditions—the big gambles, I guess you could call them. . . . But as far as me worrying about getting my crops in—if I'm sick or something, I know that there is somebody that will take over."

Neighbors like that are hard to find in a big city. City people may not have the hardships of the Iowa farmer, but that doesn't mean that they're better off. When times get tough, Iowa's farming families know they won't be alone. "It's very comforting to know that things can be carried on without you for a while," said Denny. That's just the way things are done on Iowa farms.

Harvesting the Art

There is more than corn growing in Iowa's rich soil. Iowa's rolling farmlands have also nurtured a crop of famous writers, artists, and performers.

Iowa's best-known artist is painter Grant Wood. He portrayed Iowa's people and landscapes in simple yet precise paintings. Among his many paintings is *The Midnight Ride of Paul Revere*, which showed the New England patriot riding over an Iowa landscape. His most famous painting is *American Gothic*.

Another artist who used Iowa as a subject for his art was George Catlin. He painted many portraits of Iowa's Native Americans in the 1800s. Catlin was born in Pennsylvania but devoted most of his life to recording the lifestyles of Native Americans in Iowa and the rest of the Great Plains. One of Catlin's most famous paintings is of Keokuk, a leader of Iowa's Sauk people.

A famous Iowan who often portrayed characters from the frontier days was actor John Wayne. He was born Marion Michael Morrison in Winterset in 1907. Wayne appeared in more than 250 films

Making baskets by hand is a craft that uses techniques that have been passed down from one generation to the next.

A visit to Living History Farms gives these children a chance to try out handmade farm equipment from the nineteenth century. The guide is dressed in clothes of that era.

The National Hot Air Balloon Race, held every summer in Indianola, is one of Iowa's less traditional cultural events.

over his forty-year career. He won an Academy Award in 1969 for his role in the movie *True Grit*.

The closest Wayne really came to the Wild West was in front of movie cameras. One Iowan who actually lived in the Wild West was Buffalo Bill Cody. Born in Scott County in 1846, Cody earned his nickname when the United States government hired him to hunt buffalo to feed the workers building the Union Pacific Railroad. He was such a good shot that he killed over four thousand buffalo in his first eight months on the job. Cody later started a Wild West show that traveled the United States and Europe. The show displayed the talents of legendary people such as Annie Oakley.

Cody was far from the only showman born in Iowa. Charles Ringling, born in McGregor in 1863, formed a small traveling circus with four of his

This photo shows the original Glenn Miller Orchestra. A festival to honor Glenn Miller is held annually in Clarinda, his hometown.

brothers in 1884. The circus started out with only a horse, a bear, and a few performers, but it grew rapidly under Ringling's management. In 1907 Ringling bought Barnum and Bailey's Circus, the Ringling Circus's only major competition. Together, the Ringling Brothers and Barnum & Bailey Circus became the largest circus in the world.

Another outstanding performer, jazz cornetist and composer Bix Beiderbecke, was born in Iowa in 1903. His earliest performances were on Mississippi River showboats when he was a teenager. By his early twenties, Beiderbecke was playing with master musicians such as Louis Armstrong and King Oliver. One of his most famous songs, "Davenport Blues," is about his hometown. Beiderbecke died when he was only 28 years old. Iowans and jazz fans from across the country still honor him at Davenport's yearly Bix Beiderbecke Jazz Festival.

Trombonist and composer Glenn Miller is another famous Iowa musician. Miller had become a world renowned bandleader with his Glenn Miller Orchestra by the mid-1930s. His compositions "In the Mood" and "Moonlight Serenade" are still among the most popular big band songs. Miller led the United States Air Force Band during World War II. While traveling with the band from France to England in 1940, his plane disappeared without a trace. His music, favored among those who like dance styles from the 1930s and 1940s, is still very popular.

Another Iowa composer, Meredith Willson, was well known for his musical theater compositions in the 1950s. Willson used his hometown, Mason City, as a model for the setting of his most famous musical, *The Music Man*.

One of Iowa's most famous writers is playwright Susan Glaspell. Born in Davenport in 1882, Susan Glaspell began her career as a journalist for the *Des Moines News*. She won a Pulitzer Prize in 1930 for her play *Alison's House*. Glaspell was also known for founding the Provincetown Players in Massachusetts in 1915. This experimental theater group helped famous playwrights, such as Eugene O'Neill, begin their careers.

With writers such as Glaspell in Iowa's past, perhaps it is not surprising that hundreds of people come to Iowa each year to learn to write. The University of Iowa Writers' Workshop in Iowa City is one of the most well-known creative writing programs in the nation.

The work of two other famous Iowa writers may not be considered literature, but its popularity is undisputed. Born in 1918 twin sisters Ann Landers and

Some critics consider Susan Glaspell to be America's first dramatic playwright. She also wrote novels. Two of her best-known books are *The Morning Is Near Us* and *Lifted Masks*.

Abigail "Dear Abby" Van Buren write advice columns for newspapers across the nation. Ann's given name was Esther Pauline Friedman and Abigail's was Pauline Esther Friedman! They changed their names when they started their columns. For decades people with problems have sought the home-grown advice of these two Sioux City natives.

The Des Moines Botanical Center contains one of the largest collections of tropical, subtropical, and desert plants in the United States.

Another important cultural aspect of Iowa is its rich ethnic heritage. The Amana Colonies, founded by German immigrants in the 1850s, are the most popular example of the state's diversity. Thousands of tourists come to the colonies each year to watch craftspeople use the traditional methods of their nineteenth-century ancestors. Iowa also hosts hundreds of ethnic festivals each year, including Czechoslovakian, Norwegian, and Native American ones.

There are a number of art museums throughout the state that display works from many other cultures. Iowa also has science museums and museums of cultural history. Des Moines, Cedar Rapids, and other cities sponsor symphony orchestras and community theaters, as well.

Art continues to grow in Iowa. While Iowa's farmers provide food for the body, the state's artists nourish Iowa's spirits. A celebration of cultures within a rich agricultural heritage, Iowa should inspire artists for many years to come.

Grant Wood— American Realist

Grant Wood was born in 1891 on an Iowa farm. When he was ten years old, the family left the farm for Cedar Rapids. But straight rows of corn and rolling hills appeared in Wood's work for years.

Grant Wood's mother knew he would grow up to be an artist. She loved to tell about the drawing Grant made at age three. It was only a cluster of half-moon shapes, but Grant told her he had made a chicken. Mrs. Wood was confused by the shapes until she noticed that they matched the markings on the hens in their yard. She was sure that her son had amazing talent.

Not everyone believed that Wood was a born artist, however. In art class he once painted a watercolor scene. The artistic style of the early 1900s was to make paintings appear slightly blurry. Wood didn't follow that style. He painted sharp borders and straight, hard lines. The teacher told him that his painting was too exact and held it under a faucet to blur the lines.

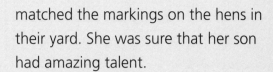

American Gothic *caused a sensation in 1930 when it was exhibited at the Art Institute of Chicago.*

This house in Eldon inspired Grant Wood to paint his most famous work, American Gothic.

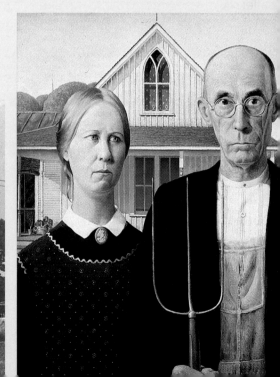

As he grew older, his reputation as an artist grew. "He was a very fine artist, but he had the common touch," Esther Armstrong, a friend of the Wood family, remembered. "Grant would take into consideration what the public thought about things."

Wood tried to show the tradition behind Iowa farm towns. His mother modeled for one of his paintings. He called it *Woman with Plants* instead of naming it after her. That way she could represent all midwestern frontier women. The plant Mrs. Wood holds in the picture is a sansevieria plant, known for its hardiness and ability to withstand rough weather. Wood explained that the plant's strength and endurance mirrored those of his mother and of all frontier women.

In 1929 Wood stopped by a plain wood house with an unusual window. He sketched the window and added two long-faced people standing in front of it, one holding a pitchfork. When he returned home, he asked his sister and his dentist to pose for the painting. One of the world's most famous paintings, *American Gothic,* was born. Wood became an almost overnight success at age 39.

Grant Wood died in 1941, and Iowans still celebrate their most famous painter yearly at their Stone City Art Festival. "[A] true art expression must grow up from the soil itself," Wood told a reporter in 1932. Grant Wood's art did just that, growing as steadily and simply as Iowa corn.

Getting Your Name in the Paper

On October 10, 1889, E. J. Sidey published the first issue of the *Adair County Democrat* of Greenfield, Iowa. He printed the newspaper's mission at the top of the first column. It stated that the newspaper would work hard to earn the confidence of the people of Adair County by devoting itself to the county's best interests. Today, the paper's name has changed—it's now called the *Adair County Free Press*. But over one hundred years after that first issue, its mission to the Adair County community is still the same. E. J.'s grandson Ed Sidey has made sure of that.

Sidey knows that crime is not the big news in a small town. It's there, of course, but what counts to the people of the town is the life they live day to day. "One of the functions, I think, of a small-town newspaper," said Sidey, "is to give everyone a spot in the news. . . . My brother once was talking to Hubert Humphrey when he was a [presidential] candidate and he said, 'The problem in the inner city is that people can be born and live and get married and die and never once have their names in the paper.' So we put their names in when they are born . . . and we run a big, long story when they are married, and we put a story on the front page when they die."

In addition somebody from the *Free Press* is at just about every special event in the county. The County Fair is one of the paper's most important events. "Our news coverage [of the fair] is mostly picture coverage," said Sidey. "And it's important to our readers that we get pictures of all those

This is the home office of the Adair County Free Press.

This cow is a winner of one of the livestock competitions at the Adair County Fair.

Three generations of Free Press publishers are shown here. They are Ed Sidey, his son Kenneth, and in the framed photo on the right, Edwin John Sidey, the paper's first publisher.

winners. Because if we don't, why, some kid is hurt. So we make a great effort to catch every one. And we always miss one, but we always try next year to score a hundred percent."

The *Free Press* has been an important part of Adair County ever since that first issue. Sidey remembers helping his father and grandfather in his youth. "[W]e used to print late at night—sometimes it was almost midnight—and still on a warm summer evening there would be a line of people standing outside, waiting for their paper."

Today, Ed Sidey has passed the paper on to his son Kenneth. His daughter Linda and son David are also part of the staff. Sidey is glad he has

been able to keep the paper in the Sidey family and make sure that his grandfather's principles have been preserved. The *Adair County Free Press* may not be the *New York Times*, but to the people of Adair County, it is just as important.

41

Steady Growth for the Future

It is unlikely that Iowa will sprout high-tech industries in its soybean fields, but that doesn't mean that industry has passed the state by. Since the late 1980s, Iowa has progressed from an entirely agricultural state to one of the most productive manufacturing states in the Midwest.

Iowa's business has been booming in the 1990s. Businesses started since 1990 grew four times faster than the national average. The state's unemployment rate averaged about two percent lower than the national average. The number of jobs in Iowa grew nearly twice as fast as the rest of the nation. Iowa is becoming more than a farming state.

One reason for Iowa's growing economy is its successful education system. Almost ninety percent of all Iowans have high school diplomas. Iowa students also score higher than any other students in the nation on the ACT and SAT college-entrance examinations. This means that Iowa's workforce is one of the best educated in the country. The state government supports

Time periods come together as Iowa's century-old capitol reflected in the mirrored-glass exterior of a modern skyscraper.

A teacher explains pottery techniques to her student. Iowa students often learn traditional crafts in addition to preparing for high-tech careers.

worker-training programs to help businesses and students across the state. The New Jobs Training Program, begun in 1983, trained or retrained almost fifty thousand workers in its first ten years.

Iowa's education is also at the forefront of technology. Electronic communications networks link the state's public schools to its universities. Young students now learn not only from their teachers but also from college professors across the state. Iowa is one of a handful of states with such advanced educational technology.

These innovative programs require a steady flow o money. One way the state has tried to raise money is by taxing riverboat gambling, which the legislature legalized in 1989. The state has also stepped up the efforts of its tourist industry. Tourists spend about two billion dollars a year in the state.

Iowa's recent advances in manufacturing, education, and tourism are helping to stabilize the state's economy by making it less dependent on agriculture. A few decades ago, most people believed that Iowa's future wouldn't reach much beyond corn and soybeans But Iowa surprised everyone with its growth. The support for a bright future is now firmly in place.

1673   The first Europeans to visit the Iowa region are the French explorers Louis Jolliet and Father Jacques Marquette.

1682   René-Robert Cavelier, Sieur de La Salle, claims the entire Mississippi Valley for France, naming it Louisiana.

1762   France cedes part of Louisiana, including Iowa, to Spain.

1800   Spain cedes Louisiana back to France.

1803   The United States buys Louisiana, which includes present-day Iowa, from France.

1804   Meriwether Lewis and William Clark set out to explore the land acquired in the Louisiana Purchase. They pass through the Iowa area.

1808   Fort Madison is built.

1832   Chief Black Hawk refuses to leave Illinois and goes to war with the United States. Army troops defeat Black Hawk, killing nearly all of his party.

1834   Present-day Iowa becomes part of the Michigan Territory.

1836   The United States government creates the Wisconsin Territory, which includes present-day Iowa.

1838   The Iowa Territory is created.

1846   Iowa is admitted to the Union as the twenty-ninth state on December 28.

1857   Iowa adopts its present constitution. A band of Sioux kills over thirty settlers near Spirit Lake in March. The Fox buy some of their former Iowa land back from the government.

1861   The Civil War begins. Iowa sends 75,000 soldiers to fight for the Union.

1868   Iowa's African American men are given the right to vote.

1869   Iowan Arabella Babb Mansfield becomes the first woman lawyer in the United States.

1880   Iowa has more than five thousand miles of railroad tracks. The state's population passes 1,600,000.

1900   The coal-mining town of Buxton is established.

1913   The Keokuk Dam is built on the Mississippi River.

1920   Iowan Carrie Chapman Catt helps convince Congress to pass the Nineteenth Amendment, which gives women the right to vote.

1930   Grant Wood's *American Gothic* is unveiled at the Art Institute of Chicago. Susan Glaspell wins the Pulitzer Prize for her play *Alison's House*.

1941   The United States enters World War II. Iowa's economy begins to recover from the Great Depression.

1960   Iowans living in cities outnumber rural Iowans for the first time.

1970s   Iowa's main economic activity switches from farming to manufacturing for the first time.

1980s   Many Iowa farmers lose their farms. Thousands of people leave the state to look for jobs. An electronic computer network connecting Iowa's schools and universities is set up.

1989   The Iowa legislature legalizes riverboat gambling in the state.

1993   Floods and frost devastate Iowa's farms. President Bill Clinton declares the entire state a disaster area.

The blue, white, and red bands on Iowa's flag represent the colors of the United States and France, both of which once owned the Iowa area. On the center white band, an eagle holds a blue ribbon carrying the state motto. The state's name is printed in red below the ribbon.

Iowa Almanac

Nickname. The Hawkeye State

Capital. Des Moines

State Bird. Eastern goldfinch

State Flower. Wild rose

State Tree. Oak

State Motto. "Our Liberties We Prize and Our Rights We Will Maintain."

State Song. "The Song of Iowa"

State Abbreviations. Ia. (traditional); IA (postal)

Statehood. December 28, 1846, the 29th state

Government. Congress: U.S. senators, 2; U.S. representatives, 5. State Legislature: senators, 50; representatives, 100. Counties: 99

Area. 56,276 sq mi (145,754 sq km), 25th in size among the states

Greatest Distances. north/south, 214 mi (345 km); east/west, 332 mi (534 km)

Elevation. Highest: 1,670 ft (509 m). Lowest: 480 ft (146 m)

Population. 1990 Census: 2,787,424 (4% decrease since 1980), 30th in population among the states. Density: 50 persons per sq mi. (19 persons per sq km). Distribution: 61% urban, 39% rural. 1980 Census: 2,913,808

Economy. *Agriculture*: corn, hogs, sheep, cattle, soybeans, oats, alfalfa, hay, apples. *Manufacturing*: food processing, nonelectric machinery, printing and publishing, electronic equipment. *Mining*: limestone, sand and gravel, clay, gypsum, coal

State Seal

State Bird: Eastern goldfinch

State Flower: Wild rose

Annual Events

★ Winter Sports Festival in Estherville (February)

★ Tulip Time Festival in Pella (May)

★ Grant Wood Art Festival in Stone City (June)

★ Scandinavian Days in Story City (June)

★ Backbone Bluegrass Music Festival in Strawberry Point (July)

★ Bix Beiderbecke Memorial Jazz Festival in Davenport (July)

★ National Hot Air Balloon Classic in Indianola (July/August)

★ Fox Indian Pow Wow in Tama (August)

★ Iowa State Fair in Des Moines (August)

★ Tri-State Rodeo in Fort Madison (September)

★ Oktoberfest in the Amana Colonies (September to October)

Places to Visit

★ Amana Colonies, near Iowa City

★ American Gothic House in Eldon

★ Buffalo Bill Museum in Le Claire

★ Effigy Mounds National Monument, near Marquette

★ Floyd Monument in Sioux City

★ Grotto of Redemption in West Bend

★ Historic General Dodge House in Council Bluffs

★ Little Red Schoolhouse in Cedar Falls

★ Living History Farms in Urbandale

★ Science Center of Iowa in Des Moines

★ Snake Alley in Burlington

★ Trainland USA in Colfax

Index